WHAT OTHERS ARE SAYING:

"*Determined Not to be Desperate* was an awesome adventure for me! I had never watched the series because I thought it might be too promiscuous for my liking. After the bible study, I felt completely different about it. This bible study made me realize that we are all so desperate for "something." The similarities between the main characters on the show and our own circle of friends are unbelievable. Krista Thomason is truly blessed by God in her ability to bring out such strong biblical points through this study...I cannot wait for Krista to write another study for the next season!"

—Nancy Boore

Kindergarten Teacher, Girard, KS

"Whether you are hearing about Christ for the first time, in the beginning stages of your faith journey, or have been a believer your whole life, you are sure to be challenged by this innovative and fresh Bible study. Krista uniquely uses a slice of pop culture as a means of reflecting God's truths. This study truly speaks to the heart of women in today's world and provides solid answers to those who may be feeling desperate. Grab a friend and get ready to enjoy!"

—Kelli McKnight

Speech Therapist, Frontenac, KS

DETERMINED NOT TO BE DESPERATE

Sandi—

Jesus is where it's at!

Kyla

DETERMINED NOT TO BE DESPERATE

TATE PUBLISHING *& Enterprises*

KRISTA THOMASON

Determined Not to Be Desperate
Copyright © 2009 by Krista Thomason. All rights reserved.

No part of this publication may be reproduced, stored in a retrieval system or transmitted in any way by any means, electronic, mechanical, photocopy, recording or otherwise without the prior permission of the author except as provided by USA copyright law.

Scripture quotations marked "NIV" are taken from the Holy Bible, New International Version ®, Copyright © 1973, 1978, 1984 by International Bible Society. Used by permission of Zondervan Publishing House. All rights reserved.

The opinions expressed by the author are not necessarily those of Tate Publishing, LLC.

Published by Tate Publishing & Enterprises, LLC
127 E. Trade Center Terrace | Mustang, Oklahoma 73064 USA
1.888.361.9473 | www.tatepublishing.com

Tate Publishing is committed to excellence in the publishing industry. The company reflects the philosophy established by the founders, based on Psalm 68:11,
"The Lord gave the word and great was the company of those who published it."

Book design copyright © 2009 by Tate Publishing, LLC. All rights reserved.
Cover design by Cole Roberts
Interior design by Jeff Fisher

Published in the United States of America

ISBN: 978-1-60799-494-7
1. Religion, Christian Life, Women's Issues
2. Religion, Christian Life, Personal Growth
09.06.29

*Thanks for believing in me, Brian.
You are my soul mate.*

CONTENTS

Introduction	11
Profiles	13
Week 1: Desperate to Conceal My Identity	15
Week 2: Desperate to Find the Truth	27
Week 3: Desperate to Control My Fear	39
Week 4: Desperate for an Identity	51
Week 5: Desperate to Have My Way	61
Week 6: Desperate to Be Better	75
Week 7: Red-Handed	89
Leader Guide and Video Discussion	93

INTRODUCTION

Everything is easier said than done. We can say we'll give up our favorite fattening food until it is put in front of our face and our craving gets the best of us. We can vow to never do something again only to turn around five minutes later and do it.

And so we deal with human nature. In Romans 7:18, 19, Paul writes about this problem saying, "I know that nothing good lives in me, that is, in my sinful nature. For I have the desire to do what is good, but I cannot carry it out. For what I do is not the good I want to do; no, the evil I do not want to do-this I keep on doing." Our spirit is willing, but the flesh is ever so weak.

Sometimes we cover our eyes to our own problems to the point of not seeing them at all anymore. It is much easier to point out others' mistakes than to confess our own.

We are all desperate for purpose, identity, love and fulfillment. I find it very easy to fill that desperation with things or people, only to be disappointed when I find out the desperation is still there. This study has the purpose of taking an honest look at ourselves, identifying our desperation, and then turning to God's Word for answers that offer true fulfillment. When we determine to put these truths into practice we no longer feel desperate.

This study uses the TV series, "Desperate Housewives" as a springboard for discussion and thought. We can identify with these ladies and the issues they face and through them we can see how we are hurting others and ultimately—God. As you go through each daily lesson on your own, identify your personal problem/sin. Look at what God has to say about it through scripture and see how and where you need to change.

Finish your time with prayer asking God for the strength to change. He's just waiting for the opportunity to work in you!

Determined—Krista

CHARACTER PROFILES

- Edie is self-sufficient and very capable. She wants everybody to know she doesn't need them and will use them to get what she wants.

- Bree is afraid of others finding out her life isn't perfect and so she puts all her focus on the external, hoping others won't notice the internal problems.

- Susan is lovable and kind, yet is impulsive and klutzy. She speaks and acts rashly and is constantly having to undo damage caused by her impulsive behavior.

- Gabrielle is interested in herself. To all those looking in on her life, she has everything. She is beautiful and married to a rich man who gives her everything she wants.

- Lynette was a super successful career woman who decided to stay at home after starting a family. She is exhausted, overwhelmed, and frustrated by the failure she feels like at home.

- Mrs. Huber is quick to point out her Christianity to others, while refusing to look at her own judgmental and superior attitude to those who aren't Christians. She uses gossip as concern for others.

All of these ladies share common ground. They are afraid if others get to know who they really are, that they will be rejected.

WEEK 1: Desperate to Conceal My Identity

Disc 1: Episode 1, "Pilot"

Day 1: *Character*

1. Look at the listed character profile. Identify how you are like each character.

   How are these traits positive?

   How are these traits negative?

2. What kinds of characteristics does God desire? Circle or highlight the characteristics God desires from the following scriptures:

Philippians 2:3–4: "Do nothing out of selfish ambition or vain conceit, but in humility consider others better than yourselves. Each of you should look not only to your own interests, but also to the interests of others."

Galatians 5:22–23: "But the fruit of the Spirit is love, joy, peace, patience, kindness, goodness, faithfulness, gentleness and self-control. Against such things there is no law."

First Corinthians 13:4–7: "Love is patient, love is kind. It does not envy, it does not boast, it is not proud. It is not rude, it is not self-seeking, it is not easily angered, it keeps no record of wrongs. Love does not delight in evil but rejoices with the truth. It always protects, always trusts, always hopes, always perseveres."

Day 2: *Crisis Management*

The episode we watched ends with the ladies agreeing that "we all find a way to survive."

1. What are some ways you survive a crisis?

2. After thinking through your survival methods, do you think they are helpful or harmful as you cope and move through a crisis?

3. Read the following scripture:

    "Elijah was afraid and ran for his life. When he came to Beersheba in Judah, he left his servant there, while he himself went a day's journey into the desert. He came to a broom tree, sat down under it and prayed that he might die. "I have had enough, LORD," he said. "Take my life; I am no better than my ancestors. Then he lay down under the tree and fell asleep.

    All at once an angel touched him and said, "Get up and eat." He looked around, and there by his head was a cake of bread baked over hot coals, and a jar of water. He ate and drank and then lay down again.

The angel of the LORD came back a second time and touched him and said, "Get up and eat, for the journey is too much for you. "So he got up and ate and drank. Strengthened by that food, he traveled forty days and forty nights until he reached Horeb, the mountain of God. There he went into a cave and spent the night."

First Kings 19:3–9

Was God angry with Elijah for being upset and even wishing to die?

Sometimes taking care of our physical needs (food and sleep in Elijah's case) minimizes the severity of the crisis in our eyes. We are also able to think more clearly as we cope and move through the crisis.

It's also normal to initially have a little pity party and even wish to die to get away from the crisis. This thought process becomes unhealthy when it continues and should be taken to a trusted friend and/or counselor.

Day 3: *Casting Stones*

Zack awakens to "the sound of a family secret." What secret(s) do you have that you desperately try to hide?

1. According to the following scripture, who is your judge?

    James 4:12: "There is only one Lawgiver and Judge, the one who is able to save and destroy. But you-who are you to judge your neighbor?"

2. According to the following verse, does God know your "secret"?

    Hebrews 4:13: "Nothing in all creation is hidden from God's sight. Everything is uncovered and laid bare before the eyes of him to whom we must give account."

3. After reading the following verse, ask yourself, *What does God think about my "secret"?*

   First John 1:9: "If we confess our sins, He is faithful and just and will forgive us our sins and purify us from all unrighteousness."

4. Read James 5:16a says, "Therefore confess your sins to each other and pray for each other so that you may be healed."

   Would it be helpful to confess your secret to a trustworthy friend?

   Although this can be a frightening thing, what benefits can come from sharing?

Day 4: *Confidential Material*

Susan and Edie are fighting for the attention of Mike. The comment is made that "women don't fight fair."

1. Does this knowledge keep us from being open with each other?

2. What other fears keep you from confiding?

3. Consider the verses below and ask yourself, *What responsibilities do I have toward a person who confides in me?*

   Job 2:11–13: "When Job's three friends, Eliphaz the Temanite, Bildad the Shuhite and Zophar the Naamathite, heard about all the troubles that had come upon him, they set out from their homes and met together by agreement to go and sympathize with him and comfort him. When they saw him from a distance, they could hardly recognize him; they began to weep aloud, and they tore their robes and sprinkled dust on their heads. Then they sat on the ground with him for seven days and seven nights. No one said a word to him, because they saw how great his suffering was."

Romans 15:1: "We who are strong ought to bear with the failings of the weak and not to please ourselves."

Galatians 6:2: "Carry each others burdens, and in this way you will fulfill the law of Christ."

Day 5: *Contentment*

Gabrielle discusses her marriage to Carlos with her fling, John. She admits that Carlos has given her everything she ever wanted. John then asks Gabrielle why she isn't happy. She responds, "It turns out I wanted all the wrong things."

We've all experienced a let down after the new wears off. We thought an item or person would bring satisfaction, yet we are still discontent.

1. Why don't things or people satisfy?

2. Why are we always longing for something more, something better, or just something else?

3. What does God say about our quest for satisfaction? Look in the following verses for your answer.

   Philippians 4:11–13; "I am not saying this

because I am in need, for I have learned to be content whatever the circumstances. I know what it is to be in need, and I know what it is to have plenty. I have learned the secret of being content in any and every situation, whether well fed or hungry, whether living in plenty or in want. I can do everything through him who gives me strength."

First Timothy 6:7–8: "For we brought nothing into the world, and we can take nothing out of it. But if we have food and clothing, we will be content with that."

Hebrews 13:5: "Keep your lives free from the love of money and be content with what you have, because God has said, 'never will I leave you; never will I forsake you.'"

Luke 12:15: "Then he, (Jesus) said to them, 'Watch out! Be on your guard against all kinds of greed; a man's life does not consist in the abundance of his possessions.'"

4. Based on these verses, how and where do you need to change in order to find contentment?

WEEK 2: Desperate to Find the Truth

Disc 1: Episode 2, "Ah, But Underneath"

Day 1: *My Truth*

Within each of us is a desire for truth. Yet there are many situations where the truth is cloudy and confusion sets in. We have to seek the truth in these situations. It may take some work on our part, we may not like what we find out, but truth is always worth it in the end.

1. Where does truth come from?

2. Does each situation decide truth or is there an absolute truth that never changes?

3. Is Jesus Christ the one true God?

4. What does the world believe?

5. What do you believe?

6. Read John 18:37–38: "You are a King, then!' said Pilate. Jesus answered, 'You are right in saying I am a king. In fact, for this reason I was born, and for this I came into the world, to testify to the truth. Everyone on the side of truth listens to me.' 'What is truth?' Pilate asked. With this he went out again to the Jews and said, 'I find no basis for a charge against him.'"

   Pilate asked the question most of us ask at one time or another: "What is truth?" If you are asking this question right now, take comfort knowing it isn't a new or wrong question to ask.

7. What problems arise when everyone decides their own truth and there is no absolute guideline?

Day 2: *God's Truth*

If we believe there is truth, we have to have something to base it on. The basis for truth has to be something more than "what I believe" or "how I was raised" or "a gut feeling."

1. Read the following verses.

> John 14:6: "Jesus replied, 'I am the Way, the Truth, and the Life. No man comes to the Father except through me.'"

> John 15:1: "I (Jesus) am the true vine and my Father is the gardener.

> John 17:3, 17: "Now this is eternal life: that they may know you, the only true God, and Jesus Christ, whom you have sent."

John 20:24–28: "Now Thomas (called Didymus), one of the twelve, was not with the disciples when Jesus came. So the other disciples told him, 'We have seen the LORD!' But he said to them, 'Unless I see the nail marks in his hands and put my finger where the nails were, and put my hand into his side, I will not believe it.' A week later his disciples were in the house again, and Thomas was with them. Though the doors were locked, Jesus came and stood among them and said, 'Peace be with you!' Then he said to Thomas, 'Put your finger here; see my hands, reach out your hand and put it into my side. Stop doubting and believe.' Thomas said to him, 'My LORD and my God!'"

Jeremiah 29:13: "You will seek me and find me, when you seek me with all your heart."

2. After reading these scriptures, how does your idea of truth change?

3. How does God's truth differ from the world's idea of truth?

God can handle your doubt and even your questions. It's okay, just don't let it end there. Earnestly seek the truth.

Day 3: *Be true to yourself*

I know myself very well. Sometimes I go to great lengths to hide who I really am because I'm afraid someone won't like me. Those yucky things I know about begin to tell me "I'm no good." Other times I think of myself as greater than I am, and I ignore my own problems and claim them as someone else's.

1. What happens when we tell a lie long enough?

2. Why is it so hard to be truthful with ourselves?

3. Romans 3:23 says: "For all have sinned and fall short of the glory of God." Based on this verse, what is the truth about humans?

4. Isaiah 64:6 says: "All of us have become like

one who is unclean, and all our righteous acts are like filthy rags; we all shrivel up like a leaf, and like the wind our sins sweep us away."

Based on this verse, is there any exemption for "good" people or are we lumped together?

5. Why is truth so important?

6. John 8:32 says: "Then you will know the truth and the truth will set you free." How does the truth set you free?

Day 4: *Be true to others*

1. Exodus 20:16 says: "You shall not give false testimony against your neighbor." Colossians 3:9 says: "Do not lie to each other, since you have taken off your old self with its practices." After reading those verses, why should we tell the truth?

   There are recorded events in scripture where a person lied and was not condemned for it.

   - Exodus 1:15–2:5 (the birth of Moses)

   - Joshua 2:1–13 (Rahab hides the spies)

   - First Samuel 21:10–15 (David acts insane)

2. Do you see the common theme in these passages?

3. In what situations would you possibly face that today?

4. Do you have to speak to lie?

Day 5: *Beyond the surface in others*

Mary Alice says that truth can be avoided because "People so rarely stop to take a look. They just keep moving."

1. Matthew 7:12 says: "So in everything, do to others what you would have them do to you, for this sums up the Law and the Prophets." After reading that verse, how should you treat others?

2. Second Corinthians 1:3–5 says: "Praise be to the God and Father of our Lord Jesus Christ, the Father of compassion and the God of all comfort, who comforts us in all our troubles, so that we can comfort those in any trouble with the comfort we ourselves have received from God."

   First John 3:16–18 says: "This is how we know what love is: Jesus Christ laid down his life for us. And we ought to lay down our lives for our brothers. If anyone has material possessions and sees his brother in need but has no pity on him, how can the love of God be in him? Dear children, let us not love with words or tongue but with actions and in truth."

After reading those verses, what are some practical ways you can begin to see the truth in others?

Suggestions: Get to know them. Offer unconditional love just as Christ offers you. Be truthful about yourself, no matter how painful it is.

3. When you say, "Hi, how are you?" are you really asking for a response beyond "fine" or "good"?

Slow down and take a look at the people around you. Inquire about their life. Be the kind of friend you would like to have. Offer more in answering another's greeting than "fine" or "good."

WEEK 3: Desperate to Control My Fear

Disc 1: Episode 3, "Pretty Little Picture"

Day 1: *My fears*

Mary Alice says, "To live in fear is not to live at all."

1. What are my fears?

2. How does your fear keep you from really living?

3. Psalm 3:6–8 says:

"I will not fear the tens of thousands drawn up against me on every side. Arise, O Lord! Deliver me, O my God! Strike all my enemies on the jaw; break the teeth of the wicked. From the Lord comes deliverance. May your blessing be on your people."

This was written by David who was running for his life from King Saul. David was surrounded by "tens of thousands," yet said, "I will not fear" and then asked God to deliver him.

How can you apply David's attitude toward his own fear in your life?

Day 2: *Control by Cover*

Look at each character, their situation, and their cover:

- Bree was afraid people would find out that she and her life aren't perfect. She covered that fear by avoiding painful issues or manipulating the situation.

- Gabrielle was afraid she would get caught in her affair. She used bribery for a cover.

- Lynette was afraid her relationship with her husband was being lost and that her parenting skills were terrible. She was honest and reached out for help.

- Susan was afraid to admit she was wrong. She covered by focusing on others' faults.

- Paul was afraid people would find out Mary Alice's secret. He covered by packing up and leaving.

- Zach was afraid his mom would be forgotten. He began to behave bizarrely.

2. Can you identify with these fears and their covers? Be honest with yourself.

3. What is the problem with trying to control our fears? Answer this based on the following verse.

   First Corinthians 3:18–20: "Do not deceive yourselves. If any one of you thinks he is wise by the standards of this age, he should become a 'fool' so that he may become wise. For the wisdom of this world is foolishness in God's sight. As it is written: 'He catches the wise in their craftiness,' and again, 'The LORD knows that the thoughts of the wise are futile.'

Day 3: *Giving Fears Away*

Maybe you are afraid of death, accomplishing your schedule, making ends meet, what other people think, etc. Those fears can have a tight hold on our lives.

1. As you read the following verses, realize God doesn't want you to live in fear, and look for the solution God offers. Write the solution after each verse.

Psalms 23:4: "Even though I walk through the valley of the shadow of death, I will fear no evil for you are with me; your rod and your staff, they comfort me."

Psalms 34:4: "I sought the Lord, and he answered me; he delivered me from all my fears."

Proverbs 12:25: "An anxious heart weighs a man down, but a kind word cheers him up."

Matthew 6:25–27: "Therefore I tell you, do not worry about your life, what you will eat or drink; or about your body, what you will wear. Is not life more important than food, and the body more important than clothes? Look at the birds of the air; they do not sow or reap or store away in barns, and yet your heavenly Father feeds them. Are you not much more valuable then they? Who of you by worrying can add a single hour to his life?"

Philippians 4: 6: "Do not be anxious about anything, but in everything, by prayer and petition, with thanksgiving, present your requests to God."

First Peter 5:7: "Cast all your anxiety on him, because he cares for you."

2. Who wants to take our fears?

3. Look at your responses from the past two days, and tell God you need his help to give your fears and anxieties to him. Every time you are tempted to be fearful, give it back to God. *He cares for you!*

Day 4: *Healthy Fear*

Confused at today's title? There is a time to fear. Really, there is a person to fear. Guess who?

1. Everyone needs to have a healthy respect (fear) for God. Find out why in the following verse. Psalms 130:3–4: "If you, O Lord, kept a record of sins, O Lord, who could stand? But with you there is forgiveness; therefore you are feared."

2. Like everything else, he doesn't ask us to do something without giving us a benefit. Check out the scriptures below. Write out the benefit of fearing God after each one.

    Proverbs 9:10a "The fear of the Lord is the beginning of wisdom."

Proverbs 10:27: "The fear of the LORD adds length to life, but the years of the wicked are cut short."

Proverbs 31:30: "Charm is deceptive, and beauty is fleeting; but a woman who fears the LORD is to be praised."

Luke 12:5: "But I will show you whom you should fear: Fear him who, after the killing of the body, has power to throw you into hell. Yes, I tell you, fear him."

3. What are some different ways we can show our fear of God?

Day 5: *When God Controls My Fear*

1. *Human Fear: Death*

   God's Freedom: Hosea 13:14: "I will ransom them from the power of the grave, I will redeem them from death . . ."

2. *Human Fear: Weather*

   God's Freedom: Nahum 1:3: " . . . His way is in the whirlwind and the storm and clouds are the dust of his feet."

3. *Human Fear: Pain/Sickness*

   God's Freedom: Revelation 21:4: "He will wipe away every tear from their eyes. There will be no more death or mourning or crying or pain, for the old order of things has passed away." (This is a reference to heaven.)

4. *Human Fear: Failure*

   God's Freedom: 1 John 1:9: "If we confess our sins, he is faithful and just and will forgive us our sins and purify us from all unrighteousness." (Not all failure is sin.)

5. *Human Fear: Loss of Possessions/Money*

   God's Freedom: Matthew 6:19–21: "Do not store up for yourselves treasures on earth where moth and rust destroy, and where thieves break in and steal. But store up for yourselves treasures in heaven, where moth and rust do not destroy, and where thieves do not break in and steal. For where your treasure is, there your heart will be also."

6. As Christians are we exempt from bad things happening? Look in the following verse for your answer. John 16:33: "I have told you these things so that in me you may have peace. In this world you will have trouble. But take heart! I have overcome the world."

7. What makes the difference when bad things happen to Christians? Answer after reading the next verse. Romans 8:28: "And we know that in all things God works for the good of those who love him, who have been called according to his purpose."

WEEK 4: Desperate for an Identity

Disc 1: Episode 4, "Who's That Woman?"

Day 1: *Who Am I?*

As I take on different roles in life, I sometimes think I've lost "the real me". Most of the time, I fail to realize "the real me" is just blossoming into something more.

1. List all your identities: (mom, wife, etc.)

2. What labels have you been given, and how are they good and bad?

3. How do you want people to identify you? Or as is often asked in old western movies, "What do you want on your tombstone?"

4. What can you do to help people identify you in this way?

Day 2: *Undercover*

One of the reasons we feel we have lost ourselves is because we think we need to be a certain way for others to like us.

1. In what ways do you become what others want you to be? After reading each verse, write out your answer.

   First Corinthians11:1: "Follow my example as I follow the example of Christ."

   First Corinthians 15:33: "Do not be misled: bad company corrupts good character."

2. When does living up to someone else's expectations become bad or harmful?

Day 3: *Read the Label!*

We've all heard or used the expression, "first impressions last." Unfortunately, many times my first impression of someone is a false assumption.

1. How is a label different from an identity?

2. When you label others, do you judge them? Consider this question as you read the following scriptures, then give your answer.

   James 2:1–4: "My brothers as believers in our glorious Lord Jesus Christ, don't show favoritism. Suppose a man comes into your meeting wearing a gold ring and fine clothes, and a poor man in shabby clothes also comes in. If you show special attention to the man wearing fine clothes and say, 'Here's a good seat for you,' but say to the poor man, 'You stand there' or 'Sit on the floor by my feet,' have you not discriminated among yourselves and become judges with evil thoughts?"

   James 2:12–13: "Speak and act as those who are going to be judged by the law that gives freedom, because judgment without mercy will be shown to anyone who has not been merciful. Mercy triumphs over judgment!"

James 4:11–12: "Brothers do not slander one another. Anyone who speaks against his brother or judges him speaks against the law and judges it. When you judge the law, you are not keeping it, but sitting in judgment on it. There is only one Lawgiver and Judge, the one who is able to save and destroy. But you-who are you to judge your neighbor?"

3. Does our perception of a person (label) always match the identity of a person?

4. Matthew 7:1–2 says: "Do not judge, or you too will be judged. For in the same way you judge others, you will be judged, and with the measure you use, it will be measured to you."

How do you measure others?

How should you measure others?

Day 4: *Identity in Christ*

We so often think that we are defined by what we do. I find it so refreshing to know that in Christ, it is all about "who" I am and not "what" I am.

Who are you? Answer this question after each scripture.

1. Psalms 139:13: "For you created my inmost being; you knit me together in my mother's womb."

2. First Corinthians 12:27: "Now you are the body of Christ, and each one of you is a part of it.

3. Second Corinthians 5:17: "Therefore, if anyone is in Christ, he is a new creation; the old has gone, the new has come!"

4. First John 3:1: "How great is the love the

Father has lavished on us, that we should be called children of God! And that is what we are! The reason the world does not know us is that it did not know him."

Day 5: *New and Improved*

It's amazing to realize how much the great God of the universe, Creator, Sustainer, Almighty (you get the idea) loves and cares about you. Not only does he love you, he believes you to be unique and shows kindness and compassion on you.

1. How does this realization change the way you feel about yourself?

Mary Alice says, "Labels are important. They dictate how we feel about ourselves."

When the world labels you as worthless, annoying, not good enough, etc., remember your identity with God. When it is all said and done, his opinion is the only one that matters. Easier said than done, but it is the truth and you need to believe it!

2. Write out the following verse on a note card, and place it on your bathroom mirror so that you can daily be reminded of who you are.

   Psalms 139:14–16: "I praise you because I am fearfully and wonderfully made; your works are wonderful, I know that full well. My frame was not hidden from you when I was made in the secret place. When I was woven together in the depths of the earth, your eyes saw my unformed body. All the days ordained for me were written in your book before one of them came to be."

3. Think of at least one or two characteristics about yourself that you can thank God for. Write those out below.

4. Take time right now to thank God for creating you just the way you are!

WEEK 5: Desperate to Have My Way

Disc 2: Episode 1, "Come In, Stranger"

Day 1: *My Way or the Highway*

1. Think of something you wanted badly, but for one reason or another it was refused to you.

2. How did you react? Upset? Angry? Defeated? Challenged? Other?

3. How important is it for you to get your way?

4. How do you go about getting your way?

5. Whether you are aggressive about getting your way, are the extreme opposite (letting others walk on you), or somewhere in between, how does your reaction affect those around you? (husband, children, friends, family, coworkers, etc.)

6. First Corinthians 13:4–5 says: "Love is patient, love is kind. It does not envy, it does not boast, it is not proud. It is not rude, it is not self-seeking, it is not easily angered, it keeps no record of wrongs."

In the space below, write out that verse, substituting your name for "love" or "it." Make the scripture much more personal by asking yourself if you are being loving.

Day 2: *Selfish or Selfless*

1. Read the following verses:

Proverbs 18:1: "An unfriendly man pursues selfish ends; he defies all sound judgment."

Galatians 5:19–20: " The acts of the sinful nature are obvious: sexual immorality, impurity and debauchery; idolatry and witchcraft; hatred, discord, jealousy, fits of rage, selfish ambition, dissensions, factions and envy; drunkenness, orgies, and the like. I warn you, as I did before, that those who live like this will not inherit the kingdom of God."

Philippians 2:3: "Do nothing out of selfish ambition or vain conceit, but in humility consider others better than yourselves."

James 3:14–16: "But if you harbor bitter envy and selfish ambition in your hearts, do not boast about it or deny the truth. Such "wisdom" does not come down from heaven but is earthly, unspiritual, of the devil. For where you have envy and selfish ambition, there you find disorder and every evil practice."

2. *Ouch!* Why are we warned so strongly about selfishness?

3. Selfishness is equated with "every evil practice" and "unfriendliness." Why?

4. Read the next two verses:

    Luke 6:38: "Give, and it will be given to you . . . For with the measure you use, it will be measured to you."

    Acts 20:35: "In everything I did, I showed you that by this kind of hard work we must help the weak, remembering the words the Lord Jesus himself said: 'It is more blessed to give than to receive.'"

5. It doesn't always immediately feel good to give up our desires or dreams for someone else's.

So, with our selfish nature in mind and these scriptures in mind, how can it be better to give than to get?

Day 3: *Give it Up!*

1. The passage below always takes my thought process away from me and my rights. Read it slowly to allow the message to penetrate your thoughts.

   Philippians 2:3–11: "Do nothing out of selfish ambition or vain conceit, but in humility consider others better than yourselves. Each of you should look not only to your own interests, but also to the interests of others. Your attitude should be the same as that of Christ Jesus: Who, being in very nature God, did not consider equality with God something to be grasped, but made himself nothing, taking the very nature of a servant, being made in human likeness. And being found in appearance as a man, he humbled himself and became obedient to death-even death on a cross! Therefore God exalted him to the highest place and gave him the name that is above every name, that at the name of Jesus every knee should bow, in heaven and on earth and under the earth, and every tongue confess that Jesus Christ is LORD, to the glory of God the Father."

2. List all the things Christ gave up for you.

3. What things did Christ gain *later* because of his selflessness?

4. Will you always see the benefits of being selfless?

5. According to this verse, what reward can you always count on?

    Revelation 22:12: "Behold, I (Jesus) am coming soon! My reward is with me, and I will give to everyone according to what he has done"

6. Back to Philippians 2 . . .

   Imagine giving up heaven to experience this earth. How does the fact that Jesus willingly gave up so much for you change your attitude about getting what you want?

Day 4: *Peace through Selflessness*

1. Have you ever made one child give a toy to another just to keep him quiet?

2. What do these verses say about keeping peace? Write out your answer in the space provided after each verse.

   Matthew 5:9: "Blessed are the peacemakers, for they will be called sons of God."

   First Thessalonians 4:11–12: "Make it your ambition to lead a quiet life, to mind your own business and to work with your hands, just as we told you, so that your daily life may win the respect of outsiders and so that you will not be dependent on anybody."

3. How do you ultimately keep peace with everyone?

4. First Timothy 2:1–2 says: "I urge, then, first of all, that requests, prayers, intercession and thanksgiving be made for everyone-for kings and all those in authority, that we may live peaceful and quiet lives in all godliness and holiness."

   After reading that verse, how can you keep peace with everyone?

Day 5: *Sneaky Selfishness or Manipulation*

1. You can manipulate a person into getting your way by bribery or by making them think it's their idea. This isn't crossing your arms and stamping your feet until you get your way, so why is it so bad?

2. Mama Solis said, "We don't cry about our problems, we find ways to fix them." This statement seems to be a good motto, but why is it so dangerous?

3. In what ways are pride and determination the same?

4. In what ways can they be different?

5. Consider the following scriptures to help you answer that question.

    Proverbs 8:13: "To fear the LORD is to hate evil; I hate pride and arrogance, evil behavior and perverse speech."

    Proverbs 16:18: "Pride goes before destruction, a haughty spirit before a fall."

    Daniel 4:37: "Now I, Nebuchadnezzar, praise and exalt and glorify the King of heaven, because everything he does is right and all his ways are just. And those who walk in pride he is able to humble."

6. Do you agree or disagree with the following statement? Why or why not?

    Pride is never good. Determination can lend itself either good or bad. Your motives and the desired end result are a good way to test yourself when deciding between pride and determination.

7. To shift the focus, I want to be sure to point out that being selfless does not mean to allow abusive behavior. Luke 17:1–2 says: "Jesus said to his disciples: 'Things that cause people to sin are bound to come, but woe to that person through whom they come. It would be better for him to be thrown into the sea with a millstone tied around his neck than for him to cause one of these little ones to sin.'"

WEEK 6: Desperate to Be Better

Disc 2: Episode 3, "Anything You Can Do"

Day 1: *My Competition*

1. Are you a competitive person?

2. In what areas of your life do you strive to win or be better than others?

Take your time thinking about this question, and be painfully honest.

3. Think about each of those areas and how you may have hurt others with your desire to be the best?

4. Ecclesiastes 2:4–11 says:

   "I undertook great projects: I built houses for myself and planted vineyards. I made gardens and parks and planted all kinds of fruit trees in them. I made reservoirs to water groves of flourishing trees. I bought male and female slaves and had other slaves who were born in my house. I also owned more herds and flocks than anyone in Jerusalem before me. I amassed silver and gold for myself, and the treasure of kings and provinces. I acquired men and women singers, and a harem as well-the delights of the heart of man. I became greater by far than anyone in Jerusalem before me. In all this my wisdom stayed with me. I denied myself nothing my eyes desired; I refused my heart no pleasure. My heart took delight in all my work, and this was the reward for all my labor. Yet when I surveyed all that my hands had done and what I had toiled to achieve, everything was meaningless, a chasing after the wind; nothing was gained under the sun."

What does the author of Ecclesiastes have to say about striving to be the best? Write out your thoughts.

Day 2: *My Best*

1. What does God expect of you? After each verse below, rephrase what it is saying that God expects of you, or underline the expectation in the scripture.

   Galatians 1:10: "Am I now trying to win the approval of men, or of God? Or am I trying to please men? If I were still trying to please men, I would not be a servant of Christ."

   Ephesians 2:10: "For we are God's workmanship created in Christ Jesus to do good works, which God prepared in advance for us to do."

   Ephesians 6:7: "Serve wholeheartedly, as if you were serving the Lord, not men."

Colossians 3:17: "And whatever you do, whether in word or deed, do it all in the name of the Lord Jesus, giving thanks to God the Father through him."

2. What makes this competition okay?

Day 3: *The Competition*

1. Answer the following questions after reading the verses.

   How can competition be beneficial?

   Hebrews 10:24: "And let us consider how we may spur one another on toward love and good deeds."

   What is the ultimate competition of life?

   First Corinthians 9:25: "Everyone who competes in the games goes into strict training. They do it to get a crown that will not last; but we do it to get a crown that will last forever."

Have you started the race?

Acts 2:37–38: "When the people heard this, they were cut to the heart and said to Peter and the other apostles, 'Brothers, what shall we do?' Peter replied, 'Repent and be baptized, every one of you, in the name of Jesus Christ for the forgiveness of your sins. And you will receive the gift of the Holy Spirit.'"

How are you doing in this race?

Hebrews 12:1–2: "Therefore, since we are surrounded by such a great cloud of witnesses, let us throw off everything that hinders and the sin that so easily entangles, and let us run with perseverance the race marked out for us. Let us fix our eyes on Jesus, the author and perfecter of our faith, who for the joy set before him endured the cross, scorning its shame, and sat down at the right hand of the throne of God.

Have you stopped?

Galatians 5:7: "You were running a good race. Who cut in on you and kept you from obeying the truth?"

Are you nearing the end of your race?

Second Timothy 4:7: "I have fought the good fight, I have finished the race, I have kept the faith."

How do I start the race for Jesus Christ?

- Believe in Him (John 3:16)

- Repent of your sins (Luke 13:3

- Confess Jesus as LORD of your life (Matthew 10:32)

- Be baptized (Acts 2:38, 1 Peter 3:21)

- Live a faithful life and produce fruit (Revelation 2:10, John 15:1–2)

For more information, talk to someone you know that is already in the race.

Day 4: *Recognizing the Success of Others*

1. Answer this question after reading each verse: *Why do I need to say nice things to others?* Write out your answer.

   Ephesians 4:29: " Do not let any unwholesome talk come out of your mouths, but only what is helpful for building others up according to their needs, that it may benefit those who listen.

   Matthew 7:12: "So, in everything, do to others what you would have them do to you, for this sums up the Law and the Prophets."

2. Again, answer this question in written form after reading the verse: *Who is the greatest?*

   Mark 9:35–37: "Sitting down, Jesus called the Twelve and said, 'If anyone wants to be first, he must be the very last, and the servant of all.' He took a little child and had him stand among them. Taking him in his arms, he said to the, 'Whoever welcomes one of these little children in my name welcomes me; and whoever welcomes me does not welcome me but the one who sent me.'"

3. Your motives come into play here also. You don't compliment to manipulate or even to get a compliment in return. According to the next set of verses, why should we "compliment" others?

    Hebrews 3:13: "But encourage one another daily, as long as it is called Today, so that none of you may be hardened by sins' deceitfulness."

    Proverbs 29:23: "A man's pride brings him low, but a man of lowly spirit gains honor."

4. Do you compare yourself, spouse, kids, etc. to others verbally or mentally?

5. Is this productive?

6. How does it make you feel when it is being done to you?

Day 5: *The Cost of Success*

Mary Alice says, "No victory comes without a price." First Corinthians 15:57 says: "But thanks be to God! He gives us the victory through our Lord Jesus Christ."

1. The ultimate victory was the cross. The cross cost Jesus a multitude of things besides pain and death. Read Matthew 26:20–70 and list the different areas Jesus was hurt (physically and mentally) before the victory came.

2. For whom are you competing?

3. For whom should you be competing?

4. Will it cost you something?

5. Will it be worth it?

WEEK 7: Red-Handed

Disc 2: Episode 4, "Guilty"

1. How do you handle getting caught in sin? Read these stories from the Bible that correspond with each housewife's situation. Identify how each Bible character and housewife handled being caught in their sin. Also, identify how you might handle each situation. Maybe you can relate to one or many of these situations. Share your experience of what did and didn't work and why.

   - Compare Bree's cover-up with 2 Samuel 11:1–17. Was Bree responsible for Andrew's selfish, non-caring attitude?

   - Mary Alice says, "Bree knew what she was about to do was wrong, but like most sinners, she would worry about her guilt tomorrow." According to Matthew 24:44, what is the problem with waiting until tomorrow?

- Compare Lynette's prescription abuse and reaching to others for help with James 5:16.

- Discuss the dialogue between the friends when they found Lynette:

- Bree says, "Nobody likes to admit we can't handle the pressure."

- Lynnette says, "Why don't we tell each other these things?"

- Answer Lynette's question.

- Compare Gabrielle's blame game with Matthew 27:24.

- Compare Carlos's soul-searching with Matthew 26:69–75.

- Compare John's guilt with Psalm 51.

- Compare Mrs. Huber's rationalization with Luke 18:9–14.

- Compare Edie's pride with 2 Kings 9:30–33.

- Compare Andrew's fear of being caught with 1 Samuel 28:1–12.

- Compare Mary Alice's suicide with Matthew 27:3–5.

2. Mary Alice says, "We all have moments of desperation. If we can face them head-on that is when we find out how strong we are." Do we have to face our desperate moments alone?

3. After going through this study and looking at the emptiness of desperate measures, let's . . .

   - ✓ Determine to be honest about *who* we are.

   - ✓ Determine to look past the surface in others.

   - ✓ Determine to stop allowing fear to control us.

   - ✓ Determine to be true to ourselves and not label others.

   - ✓ Determine to be selfless.

   - ✓ Determine to stop competing with others and compete for God.

LEADER'S GUIDE AND VIDEO DISCUSSION

Introduction	95
Worksheet: What Happens When We Die?	100
Week 1: Desperate to Conceal My Identity	103
Week 2: Desperate to Find the Truth	109
Week 3: Desperate to Control My Fear	113
Week 4: Desperate for an Identity	119
Week 5: Desperate to Have My Way	123
Week 6: Desperate to Be Better	127
Week 7: Red-Handed	131

INTRODUCTION

A Note to the Teacher:

Every situation is different. What has worked for me may not work for you. God knows each situation and everybody's needs. Depend on him to lead you through the discussions and the videos.

At the first class, I would suggest you hand out the workbooks and explain that they are personal and will take about five minutes each day to accomplish. Each week is divided into five days and *follows the video instead of leading up to the next week's video.* Also explain that you will take about ten minutes to go over the workbooks at the beginning of each class time but that you will not ask for them to share their dirty laundry. Their privacy will be respected.

At the next six classes, begin with workbook discussion, move to the video, then close with video discussion. I would read scriptures and pray instead of asking for others to do this. If you have unchurched or new Christians, they will be extremely intimidated thinking they may be called on. You don't want to lose someone over that.

All videos are from season one, discs one and two. I would strongly suggest that you watch each video beforehand to be familiar enough to know if you need to skip parts. Keep in mind that you want to watch enough of the video to be able to have a good discussion. Also, the narrator of the show has committed suicide and "watches" her friends from the dead. I have included a worksheet in your guide on "What happens when we die?" You may want to use this, as there is a lot of worldly confusion on life after death.

This is not a clean show. There is adultery, murder, lies, gossip, backbiting, filthy language, etc. Unfortunately, I've realized that in the church we will accept gossip, backbiting, jealousy, little white lies, but shun the adulterers and other *big* sins. This show has captured the minds and hearts of many women worldwide. Why not use it to teach who Jesus is and what he has to say about life? Read Acts 17:16.

As Christians we are called to be separate and holy and most often we interpret that as staying away from the "sinners." I have realized that my mind and actions must be holy, but the only way I'm going to reach others for Jesus is to be around them physically. That means being culturally relevant.

Paul says it best in 1 Corinthians 9:22: "I have become all things to all men in order that I might win some."

For each class you will need:

1) Leader's Guide (answers to questions are in italics)

2) Student Workbook

3) *Desperate Housewives* video taken from season one, discs one and two. you can purchase, rent, or borrow this. The beginning of each lesson will tell you which video to show for that particular class.

4) A Bible, including extras for those who may not have one.

5) Pens

CLASS FORMAT:

Week 1: video, video discussion
Week 2: homework discussion, video, video discussion
Week 3: homework discussion, video, video discussion
Week 4: homework discussion, video, video discussion
Week 5: homework discussion, video, video discussion
Week 6: homework discussion, video, video discussion
Week 7: homework discussion, video, video discussion

What happens when we die?

1)   Read Hebrews 9:27.

- We die.

- Then we wait for judgment.

2.   Revelation 20:11–15.

- The dead are held until judgment.

3.   Read Luke 16:19–31.

- If your Bible uses the word hell in verse twenty-three, it is the Greek word (the original Bible was written in Greek) for Hades. Hades is the waiting place of the dead. Hades is divided into two compartments:

- One compartment is paradise. Those awaiting judgment can then go to heaven.

- The other compartment is torment. Those awaiting judgment then go to hell.

- Verse twenty-six of Luke chapter 16 says there is a chasm between the two that cannot be crossed. So, the dead are not able to roam as spirits.

- Verse thirty-one says the dead are not allowed to go back.

- When is judgment?

- Second Peter 3:10

- After Christ returns to earth

- How does God feel about mediums?

- Leviticus 20:27 tells us God expected them to be killed for their practice.

- Deuteronomy 18:10–12 tells us God detests the practice of mediums.

- If mediums aren't seeing the dead, then what are they seeing?

- Second Corinthians 11:14

- First Timothy 4:1

- Revelation 16:14

These verses tell us that Satan and his demons are out to deceive us. They are the ones roaming the earth.

7. Should we fear the devil and demons?
First John 4:4 tells us that, no, we should not fear the devil and demons. They fear Jesus, who is in us.

Week 1: Desperate To Conceal My Identity

You will need Disc 1, Episode 1, "Pilot" for the video discussion.

1. Read this quote to your group:

    "I spent this day as any other, quietly polishing the routine of my life until it gleamed with perfection."–Mary Alice

2. Ask the following questions to generate discussion. Possible answers are in italics.

    - What exactly does that mean? *Making the outside look perfect to others*

    - On the way to the wake, we find out how each character polishes their life to perfection. What are Gabrielle and Carlos doing to polish? Keep in mind the following response by Gabrielle to Carlos after he berated her for raising her voice in front of others: "We wouldn't want them to think we're not happy."

- *They were putting up a front to make others think they were in a happy marriage.*

- How about Lynette? *She bribes her children with Santa in hopes of good behavior.*

- What does Susan do? *She brings her one dish, mac 'n cheese, and then tosses it as soon as everyone saw she brought something.*

- Bree spends a lot of time making sure her life looks good. What were some of the things she did all by herself? *Cooking, sewing, gardening, re-upholstering, etc.*

3. What is each character trying to hide?

    - Gabrielle and Carlos–*unhappy marriage*

- Lynette–*undisciplined boys which reflects on her mothering ability*

- Susan–*coming empty handed.* Why bother bringing a dish when you know nobody will eat it? *We don't want people to think we aren't pulling our weight.*

- Bree–*the fact that she isn't perfect*

4. Read the following verses to see what God has to say about making the outside look perfect?

    - 1 Samuel 16:7

    - Matthew 23:27

5. Read this quote to the group:

    - "Everyone thought of Bree as the perfect wife and mother, everyone except for her family."–Mary Alice

6. Those closest to us see right through our appearances. What kinds of things do we do for appearance sake at their risk?

7. What burdens do we carry by being one way and acting another?

8. Do we take care of others to the point of neglecting our own family? Why? Is it our own expectations or others'?

9. What does God have to say about taking care of family, according to 1 Timothy 5:8?

10. Read this quote to the group:
    "Sometimes people pretend to be one way on the outside when they are totally different on the inside."–Susan

11. Let's look at a couple of situations and discuss why we hide who we are.

    - Lynette is at the grocery store and runs into an ex-co-worker. She asks Lynette if motherhood is the best job she ever had. "To those who asked Lynette this question, there was only one acceptable answer, so she lied."–Mary Alice

- *Lynette feels like a failure. She doesn't want this co-worker, who knows her as extremely successful, to see that she feels like a failure at motherhood.*

- Bree runs into Mrs. Huber at the salad bar. Mrs. Huber asks her how she is doing. "Bree longed to share the truth about her husband's betrayal, but for Bree, admitting defeat was not an option."–Mary Alice. *Bree lets her pride keep her from honesty.*

12. How can we hold our head up and be honest if we're in a situation like this?

    Read Colossians 3:23 and Proverbs 8:13. Discuss what God has to say in relation to these situations.

13. What keeps us from being honest with each other? *Fear of being rejected.*

14. Read the following quote from Mary Alice:

    "We all have moments of desperation, if we can face them head-on, that is when we find out how strong we are."

15. How is this true?

16. Do we have to do it alone?

17. Read Exodus 17:8–13.

    - Only Moses could fight this battle, but he had friends come along beside to hold up his hands and help him be more comfortable while he fought.

    - We all feel like failures at different times. We don't want others to see that we can't "handle" our situation. If we would be honest with each other, we can help each other through difficulties.

18. Pray with your group to end your discussion time.

Week 2: Desperate to Find the Truth

You will need Disc 1, Episode 2, "Ah, but Underneath" for the video discussion.

"People so rarely stop to take a look, they just keep moving"–Mary Alice

1. The theme for this video is seeing what you want to see. Read Mark 10:13–16

    The disciples thought the children were a distraction, but Jesus saw beyond the surface and the here and now. He took the time to love people.

2. Think back to the video: Who was able to see beyond the surface to the truth in others?

    Dr. Goldfine with Bree, and Susan with Mike

3. Who chose not to look beyond the surface?

   Susan with Gabrielle (Susan is suspicious but wants to believe the best about her friend.)

   Lady with Lynette (She already made up her mind about Lynette's parenting skills.)

   Police officer with Lynette (The officer didn't want to have to listen)

   Rex with Bree (He believes it all to be Bree's fault. He chose not to see the truth about himself.)

   Carlos with Gabrielle (Mary Alice says,"What he couldn't see, couldn't hurt her.")

4. Keeping the housewives in mind, think of personal examples of when we choose not to dig deeper for the truth.

   Suspicious, but wants to believe the best (*our children*)

   Mind is already made up (*allowing gossip and judgment to decide*)

Don't want to listen *("Hi, How are you?" without waiting for response)*

Blaming everything on the other person *(spouse, employee, employer, finances)*

5. Lynette is honest and tries to reach out for help but is ignored by the police officer and judged by the lady. What does God have to say about judging others? Read James 4:11–12

6. How often do we make correct judgments about others?

7. Being concerned for others can border on being nosy. What would make the distinction between the two? *Motive and gossip sessions (sometimes disguised as prayer requests)*

8. Gabrielle tells Carlos to take her breath away. Carlos buys her a car. Did he understand what she was asking for?

9. Have you ever had a similar situation? Does

your husband always understand your need(s)? How do you handle that?

10. Mary Alice ends the show by saying, "Loneliness was something my friends understood all too well." We all feel lonely and left out at times, maybe more often than not. Guess what? You're in good company. Read Isaiah 53:3–4. It hurts, but at those times remember that Jesus knows *exactly* what you are feeling and lean on him for comfort. On the other hand, make sure you aren't the one allowing someone else to be lonely. Take time to look beyond the surface in others.

Week 3: Desperate to Control My Fear

You will need Disc 1, Episode 3

"Pretty Little Picture" for the video discussion.

I would suggest viewing all of this episode, except to skip after Bree calls everyone to the table.

1. Discuss the statement made by Mary Alice, "To live in fear is not to live at all."

   Some of the things we fear are beyond our control (storms, death). When we spend time worrying about things we have no control over, we waste our time.

   Some of our fears can be controlled (marriage issues to a degree, letting go of anger, etc.). When we refuse to let the fear go, we waste our time.

2. We've seen countless movies about people who are dying. Usually when they find out they are dying they make a list of things to do. Why is that?

3. Why does death make us want to live?

4. Are we assured of the next minute of our life?

5. What are the advantages to living as if we might die tomorrow?

6. What are the disadvantages to living that way?

7. How can we find a happy medium?

8. Psychologists say people have two responses to fear: fight or flight. Look at the following situations the housewives are in and decide if that particular housewife is choosing a "fight" or "flight" response.

- Lynette is afraid their marriage might not be good or that they aren't happy. What is her response? *Fight–She discusses it with Tom who in turn "tries."*

- Gabrielle is afraid of her affair coming "out of the closet". What is her response to the little girl who caught her kissing John? *Fight–She bribes the girl with a bike and then teaches her to ride it.*

- Paul is afraid of people finding out why Mary Alice killed herself. What is his response? *Flight–He puts his house on the market.*

- Zach is afraid of forgetting his mom. What is his response? *Fight–He confronts his dad about the obituary and the gun.*

- Bree is afraid of people finding out about her troubled marriage. What is her response? *Flight–She refuses to let anyone know they are in counseling, even to the point of concocting the tennis story.*

9. Susan is afraid of admitting she was wrong. At first, she refused to let go of her anger, taking a flight from the truth. But then she fights and apologizes to her ex and his girlfriend. What happens when she apologizes? *She feels much better, and she gets an apology from Brandi. It felt good.*

10. Let's settle here and talk about forgiveness. Susan says, "I've lived with this bitterness so long, I think I'd be lonely without it."

    What does she mean? *Sometimes our hurts and bitterness offer a bit of comfort and something to talk about with others.*

11. How does God forgive you and me? Psalms 13.:12

12. Read Matthew 6:14, and Matthew 5:21–22a.

Does God expect us to forgive people who wrong us?

13. Whose behavior can we control? *Our own. Many times when we make positive changes in ourselves and treat people with respect, we begin to see a change in them also.*

14. Finish your discussion with prayer time.

Week 4: Desperate for an Identity

You will need Disc 1, Episode 4, "Who's That Woman?" for this video discussion.

1. Read the following to the group:

"Labels are important, they dictate how we see ourselves."–Mary Alice

2. What is the difference between your identity and being labeled? *An identity is who you are, while being labeled is what others think you are.*

3. How often does our perspective change about someone else after we've experienced something similar to them or walked in their shoes?

   How have each of the characters been labeled?

- Lynette ... *unable to control her children*

- Susan and Edie ... *each thinks the other is throwing themselves at Mike*

- Paul ... *dark, malignant*

- Mike ... *that he wants a woman*

- The twins' teacher ... *unable to handle her class*

- Bree ... *double standards*

- Twins ... *ADHD*

- Dancers ... *troubled childhood*

5. Were labels given to each of these characters before or after all the information concerning them was received? *Before*

6. When you label somebody, what are you doing? *Judging them*

7. Genesis thirty-eight records an interesting story about someone who was labeled but redeemed herself. Read or paraphrase this story to the group.

8. Close your time together with prayer.

Week 5: Desperate to Have My Way

You will need Disc 2, Episode 1, "Come In, Stranger" for this discussion.

1. The following quote by Gabrielle is the main theme of this discussion. Read it to your group. "You're a woman. Manipulate him. That's what we do."

2. Discuss how does each character manipulates another?

    - Bree with Rex and Zach? *food*

    - Gabrielle with John? *sex*

    - Gabrielle with Mama Solis? *shopping*

    - Lynette with her twins? *"fun" activities to wear them out*

- Lynette with Tom? *Reminder of her sacrifice for the boat*

- Officer with Susan? *Told her what she wanted to hear*

- Mama Solis with Gabrielle? *threat*

- Susan with Mike? *goes on date with police officer*

3. What is manipulation? *It is basically control.*

4. What are negative outcomes from control? *Bitterness, rebellion, not allowing others to be themselves. Others don't want to be around a control-freak*

5. Mostly, these are examples of manipulation being bad, but how can it be good? *Education, parenting, etc.*

6. What determines whether it is good or bad? *Your intent. Are you trying to get your way or educate?*

7. Read the story of Samson and Delilah in Judges 16:1–2.

8. How did Delilah manipulate Samson? How was Delilah manipulated?

9. Finish your discussion with prayer.

Week 6: Desperate to Be Better

You will need Disc 2, Episode 3, "Anything You Can Do" for this discussion.

1. Read the theme of this discussion as quoted by Mary Alice: "Rule # 1–In order to win, you have to want it more."

2. How does each character try to outdo another?

    - Tom with his sales pitch–*He brings clients to his home so the other guy won't be there to make him look bad.*

    - Lynette–*She steals meds so she can keep up with demands and "do it all."*

    - Susan–*She throws her date in Edie's face and the bull ride to compete with Kendra for Mike*

- Edie–*She wants to steal Mike from Susan, not Kendra*

- Gabrielle–*She sponsors Danielle to go to New York to keep her away from John*

- Paul–*He wants to take out the person who drove Mary Alice to suicide*

- Rex–*He gives big gifts to kids*

- Bree–*She throws kids out of house if they don't go by her rules (give back gifts)*

3. Why do we find comfort in being "just a little better" than another person?

4. Read this quote: "Whether a friendly rivalry or a fight to the death, there is the same end result, there are winners and there are losers."–Mary Alice

5. Read Mark 10:35–45.

6. Jesus says to be the greatest, you must be a servant. How should this change our view on being better?

7. Discuss the following statement by Mary Alice with your group:"The trick is to know which battles to fight."–Mary Alice

8. End your discussion time in prayer.

Week 7: Red-Handed

You will need Disc 2, Episode 4, "Guilty" for this discussion.

1. You will find the video discussion in the "Determined . . ." workbooks. You will all do this together. There is no daily study for this final week.

2. There won't be enough time to read every story, so you will need to become familiar enough with each passage to be able to give a good summary to everyone.

3. The Bible has the original stories of desperate people. It also tells us how to leave desperation behind and live abundantly.

4. The key verse to this discussion (not in the workbooks) is Numbers 32:23. Paraphrasing this verse, it says, "Be sure your sins will find you out!"

5. Finish your study with prayer.